THE PACIFIC NORTHWEST POETRY SERIES

Linda Bierds, General Editor

THE PACIFIC NORTHWEST POETRY SERIES

2001   John Haines   *For the Century's End*

2002   Suzanne Paola   *The Lives of the Saints*

2003   David Biespiel   *Wild Civility*

2004   Christopher Howell   *Light's Ladder*

2005   Katrina Roberts   *The Quick*

2006   Bruce Beasley   *The Corpse Flower*

2007   Nance Van Winckel   *No Starling*

2008   John Witte   *Second Nature*

2009   David Biespiel   *The Book of Men and Women*

2010   Christopher Howell   *Dreamless and Possible*

2011   Katrina Roberts   *Underdog*

2012   Kathleen Flenniken   *Plume*

2013   Nance Van Winckel   *Pacific Walkers*

2013   David Biespiel   *Charming Gardners*

2014   John Witte   *Disquiet: Poems*

2015   Christianne Balk   *The Holding Hours*

2017   Kevin Craft   *Vagrants & Accidentals*

2017   Melissa Kwasny   *Where Outside the Body Is the Soul Today*

WHERE OUTSIDE THE BODY IS THE SOUL TODAY

MELISSA KWASNY

UNIVERSITY OF WASHINGTON PRESS

Seattle & London

Where Outside the Body Is the Soul Today, the eighteenth volume in the Pacific Northwest Poetry Series, is published with the generous support of Cynthia Lovelace Sears.

Copyright © 2017 by the University of Washington Press
Printed and bound in the United States of America
Design by Katrina Noble
Composed in Scala, typeface designed by Martin Majoor
21 20 19 18   5 4 3 2

UNIVERSITY OF WASHINGTON PRESS
www.washington.edu/uwpress

LIBRARY OF CONGRESS CATALOGING-IN-PUBLICATION DATA
Names: Kwasny, Melissa, 1954– author.
Title: Where outside the body is the soul today / Melissa Kwasny.
Description: Seattle : University of Washington Press, [2017] | Series: Pacific
    Northwest poetry series |
Identifiers: LCCN 2017017193 (print) | LCCN 2017022855 (ebook) |
    ISBN 9780295742458 (ebook) | ISBN 9780295742441 (hardcover : alk.
    paper)
Classification: LCC PS3561.W447 (ebook) | LCC PS3561.W447 A6 2017 (print)
    | DDC 811/.54—dc23
LC record available at https://lccn.loc.gov/2017017193

To Bryher

The greater part of the soul is outside the body.
—MICHAŁ SĘDZIWÓJ

CONTENTS

WHERE
OUTSIDE
THE BODY
IS THE SOUL
TODAY

The book begins, rightly, with the Killing Floor. A pig has skin that most resembles ours, having no membrane between it and its *flesh and blood*. The skin must be cooled, the heat of life in it. One must put away the vodka, the salt. Whether smooth skinned or blue feathered or shining with fur, underneath each of us, gristle and brine. Aging, the hair slip on the cowhide. Swelling knees, our scars, our tattooed stains—each year so long we find ourselves confronted with it. Sitting in the dirt becoming mud of the sweating house. Windows of the body, how to clear them? The Yupiit break the ice from the waterholes so the sea mammals can see them. Wild orchids seed in clutches under the fir, facing east. We look forward to silk and trees, to the court life. Snow melts. Sun rises, as if under a spell.

I.

THE DEER PEOPLE

THE DEER PEOPLE

Stumbled under the shade of birds. Scratched a little hollow
in the dirt and hid the rings there.

Moved quiet and alone among the others. As if through snow.
Wearing the sage wristbands.

Considered sunshine and its synonyms. Considered its antonym:
the ebbing tide. Spot-lit, entered from the wings.

Stepped into a spirit world where the natural show themselves.
Wearing a guise of the same.

"disconnected" "little dreams" "false continuum" (Alice Notley).
Often a complete and common shyness.

To candle is to examine an egg's freshness by holding it to the light.
Hole in the ozone. Hole in the soul's tallow lining.

That grown men can hold their guns to the soft belly of a child.
That they can shoot someone who is so afraid.

The violence we have allowed to blow through us. Locked
bedroom door bucking in its casement.

Considered peace and its synonym. The whitetail doe and her fawn.
Crossed the field of the mind meadow-wise.

To ask a question is a promise that one will listen. How the fir is within the fire. Wind in the windrow.

Saw not particulars but glow. Fed off the nose. Cleared the air of all but the smell of clover.

THE PRONGHORN ANTELOPE PEOPLE

Antholops, a Greek name. Intermediate between goat
and wind. "Little horse" to the academics.

We are mirrors. Let the past imagine us.
It cannot be entertained. It is large, like an owl landing.

In the guidebook, the smooth green snake that crossed
my path is named the Smooth Green Snake,

in the story, which I have been invited to take a part in.
In the circle of intimates, which include the deer.

The Cheyenne word for tea: a flower soup, a soup of leaves.
The antelope mime for us the tragedy

of a language besieged, bounding past our industries,
jumping in the snowmelt stream,

falling back in their efforts to mount the bank. World view.
In theirs, few of us exist. A function of eyes

placed sideways so they have to sidle to see ahead.
Hip tricked against the highline. A solitary atop the ridge.

The blue sage whispers to the rattlesnake, coiled around
its stem to escape the heat.

Breakfast, a brewing fest of coolness. Morning fog, a feather down. Winter burr. Summer rapids.

The antelope emerge from the seed-holes of evening: gully, coolie, draw. Loosely beaded, an elastic string.

Their cloud design, all eyebrow. All shade unto themselves. Color of rabbit tail and bone meal.

We could hunt them down, but then they would be dead. We don't discover them. They cross our paths,

ancestral members of a world we lost, the terra cotta shards of a vein. Coal seams set on fire by lightning.

THE WIND PEOPLE

Wind people, like the buffalo,
are indigenous to our plains and demand the same fate,

the same reprisals. Burial after burial,
incremental, so that often we are too late to attend them.

But the sound of grief breaks.
The whimpering begins. The build-up, the acceleration.

Every known culture has taken upon itself
naming of the soul, usually in words for smoke or wind.

It slows us down the road in its direction.
Tourists return from the famous battlefield, chastened.

Where do the ghosts go, are they shouldering these gusts,
or, slipping our senses, do they bunker

floor-length, stooped over us but lost from our thoughts?
Who is it that manages the heavy lifting.

To lament, honor, feel shame. The composer
asks if there is a word that includes both apology and praise.

Confession perhaps, a plea for absolution. An open screen.
The shape of our violence somehow heard by us.

THE COTTONWOOD PEOPLE

Faint. Uncombed. Awash in rain.
They share the kind of beauty shared by older women.

Rhapsody in wind. Buds,
not leaves: the small greens crowding up behind them.

Music, if one could see it, its wicker, its cursive strain.
Spruce, which has the heavier sails, flapping.

You are everything you feel beside the river. (Seamus Heaney)
Through the silver-paned bark, the diamond pores of

sloughed-off skin. If I saw my soul, she would be this tree,
and I would love her.

Placing stops between the strings, a composer
warps the score though making noise is never the intention.

One can draw anything on paper and ask a musician to play it.
For instance, a violinist known for her sheer nerves.

It is good to be cold, to remember cold. Hushed by rain,
to be ordained in a dry place. Suppleness of the word *posture.*

By the time my friend received the diagnosis, she was no longer
prepared to accept it—

  an afterimage shot with stores of pollen.

THE ASPEN PEOPLE

The heavy early snow that came
when leaves were green
bent willows and alders to earth,
broke the waistlets of yellow pine,
but worse, snapped in half
the plumy aspens near the roadside.

Ascetic. Thin and resonant,
thus, tragic. What we mean essentially
when we say someone is *too sensitive*.
They fall through air. They crack.
Leaving the hours open without plan.

Leaves click and murmur below me
like pebbles on shore when the outgoing tide
passes through them, reminding me
that air is fluid.
I can wipe it across my cheeks,
anointed with dust as I was as a girl.

This is not a life of quiet correspondences.
Not the life we thought we were here to live.
But it survives, a step behind us.
Two shining cups, though three have spilled.

THE DEER PEOPLE AGAIN

Tethered to each other so lightly,
so as not to call attention to the self.
Reassess. The morning a soft kiss,
but now the wind is back, unnerving all of us.
Who came that brought it with them?
The gray ones, the other side.
Kindness must be the mediator here.
I am a stone plunked into Grass Lake.
The deer dilate into twins,
the width of their radiance contingent
on how fast or slow I am walking.
Green tablet inside the tablets of darker green.
I am working on my resonance.
The theme is touch. Transfiguration of matter
that can occur through wonder.
What's ahead? What is its shape? Is it dangerous?
Deer ask the same questions we do.
To be alert to the extraneous and yet miss
the most obvious cues: headlights,
the crush of tires on pavement.
And more ancient—people arranging their days
to travel from one ceremonial site to another.
As all days are ceremonial.
The deer come alive in the sunset hour,
from far away, from outside our lives.
A ghost might come and stand in just this way.
As if it were watching me from behind thick glass.
As if it thought it were invisible to me.

II.

ANOTHER LETTER TO THE SOUL

1.

You are the story of my love in ruins, the garden I planted in what was left of the concrete. You are the back step of childhood, mother and father so absorbed in each other their children were like ants got into the kitchen, a nuisance, an insignificant grief. Let me start there. My pilot light, you led me out. I recognized you first in the side yard, in the hard-packed solitude where the roses grew. In my long adolescence, you taught me to bear the heavy self, like carrying loads in one's arms of wet laundry. But what are your attachments? I feel as if I belong to you, but you belong to something else. You are older than me, wiser, more well-connected. What now, I know I keep asking. What should occupy me in these last days? Day air in the clearing, lifelong friend of trees, it is possible that you direct the full itinerary. Arboretum of the unclaimed versos of the leaf.

2.

You picked me from the litter as a brightness, rubbed me between finger and thumb. You placed me, and the bees, who are like-spirits, came. You gave them, through me, a place to come to. You provided me with properties, inaudible spells, invisible arrows that point to the hurt places. Illness of my friends: her failing liver, his failing nerves, earth-drought, flood, the poisoned animal. I know you have been testing me, first toughening the fragile frame. Inside, an infant cries and objects. You kept me apart like the bald eagle found floundering in the river and put into the feeding cage. Long enough to gain its strength back, and then it fled. I admit I didn't know that a broken wing could right itself. I forget about healing, though I grow fonder of birds, the poor nieces I can afford to bring the berries to. Sun's out, you say, serving its broth of light.

3.

The watercolorists are happy. They've picked their views and are sitting, barely moving, in long-sleeved shirts. Mystery *and clarity* is what they aim for as an achievement. You speak in the variations of wind. Upper reaches of the cottonwood, its adolescent limbs spurred on and off into a froth of soundings. Anxiety of ground-shadows as wind passes among the leaves. It stops, and the tiny insects descend. We experience you only in your arrivals, not departures, so strong you tear the tent from our hands. And yet your remains are tender, broken and soft, as if strung with beads of dew atop wet sand. Each one of us suffers, small things and joys. All of us are aging, having watched each other age. What are the past lives of the wind? It cycles through the channel where the deer carcass stinks. Where dinosaur bones protrude from the ancient banks.

4.

You are the sound of rain, if it weren't falling but rising from below, a ground-nester, not a tree one, such as the bobolink or longspur, created below our feet, like the oil is. Rain in the ears and snowmelt rushing through the heart, a distant sound, as of the past retreating. Though loud, continuing its retreating presence. What can the flood teach me about you? I see frothing at the surface and watch myself pulled in, as if identity were an antithesis to gravity. Yet not knowing is part of you, whether I sink or swim, whether I abandon the body or stay and fight for it. When someone says, "you will know when the time comes," does she mean the soul speaks? What part, then, indecision, net of doubts we might call debris, web of plastic tape roping off the danger? Mudbanks where the deer's leg sinks in?

5.

Water. Mint. Water-mint. The braided currents at the bend of the nearby stream. Their fluid consonance. The granite boulder, like a sibyl behind summer leaf, shade-spattered with lichen and moss. Gaston Bachelard writes that, in human reverie, *the rock imagines*. Not that we imagine the rock. How could we have come here, have accepted so much, without having had a foundation to build on? So, soul as luggage, our library, perhaps our DNA? *Entrance* as noun: what we step through. *Entrance* as verb: how we are changed. What could we see if not movement? The sibyl measures each fish's weight against the blue root of her own. The leafage separates in autumn into its individual tones. We say autumn moves us. That it is moving. Given the forecast. Given how easily the subject can be erased.

6.

I am working out the days of the week, their attributes and powers. Today is the day of the dead again. On Tuesdays, I am heron, over-tall, marked by blue, so quiet in public I am barely perceptible. Tree days, during which I whisper and don't answer the phone. I woke up one morning and vowed to practice: days when I am creek bed, taking naps and sleeping long. There are naturally certain strains I have to bend to. Perhaps you reveal yourself as I get older, though you become harder to define, bedding yourself down, flattening the grasses. Like the deer under the cherry tree, gone at first light, yet, in late September, moving ever closer to the house. On deer days, I am alert for traffic, ready to abandon the road, remind myself to stay close to those who follow. Though it is not in the mind that I want to venture out. I enjoy your references, the laying out of the picture cards, but it is the exterior where the vision must be enacted.

III.

THE BLUE HERON PEOPLE

THE BLUE HERON PEOPLE

I send *artemesia* to my sister, its silver coolant
for her fever,
and a winding sheet of lilac and blue flax,
whose colors wash out in the rains,
for her pain. Denim and chambray of the heron.

How do we position ourselves against
the ancestors in the blood? Change one thing
and the rest will follow.
Our voices, the American Indian writer said,
are ugly to the birds and snakes.
We should instead think our thoughts to them.

On weekends, trucks head into the mountains,
loaded with trailers and ATVs,
with their heaviness, with their violent expense.
Animals dilate, the grasses suffer.

But what is *our* true nature, our essential form?
At half their future height, the heron chicks
stand in their high nests, staring out
at us, at danger, from atop their twiggy necks,
not realizing how obvious they are.

We were not a pretty family. We were raw.
I send my sister the blue wheat grass, flowering
into its elegant art deco scrolls,

the shade fir trees hold, close, below their limbs.
I send her distance, the serious flight of herons:

They who have inherited the water traits. Who wade
through mint. They, who are better left alone.

YELLOW POND LILY

Green ibis, a flock of white egrets. Box turtles dozing in the sun. And then, two alligators, small and torpid, segmented like medieval mail, curving chains in the backyard canal. All this to say that creatures come to us, showing themselves because they can, unlike to those too busy or minds too worried. We need them as my mother needs to hold her little dog, bending over him on her lap as she prays each morning. Great Gentleness, healer of travesties, my mother's back is in pain, having carried lifelong my father's meanness and madness—keeping the lost one found, the damaged boat afloat because that is what humans do: reach out to the needy. When you touch plants or people, the Cheyenne medicine man said, touch them as if they were a god. You would not take god's hand and shake it vigorously. But what if my father did? If I do?

THE ROCK PEOPLE

Shut inside the summer house, the rock
has disappeared. All glower, the shallow-work of leaves.

A bower contains the impulse to bow to it,
contains a bow, which bows also, bent to a tension, a string.

There is a perfume about it, the perfume of leisure—
chokecherry, river birch, red willow.

Which is not visible, but sensible, entering mind
like a thought. Thought from minor gods, inflorescences.

My parents taught me to work hard, to buy secondhand,
go for the sale. To bow to money

but also loyalty to family, as in "the human psyche"
"made of women" "turned to stone" (Alice Notley).

Or should I say "bone"? The dead string our bloodlines.
They pause inside the stream. Time, the *sense of time*—

we are set into it by other hands.
A second hand for consciousness we name the cursive.

The sky is worldly, large and moving, with moving
and large clouds. I have been here long, not long enough

to have traversed it. Did anyone know
to say your life is finite, that *here* is called earth,

that our species was not first, or even early? That plants
do not bloom for us but to perpetuate their kind.

That miles below our feet an inner fire is burning?
But, of course, my parents didn't know.

THE RED-WINGED BLACKBIRD PEOPLE

I can live with heresiarchs. I like the *here* in them and the *arch*,
the about-face, a bright badge
tossed back and forth across the fields of the party's faithful.

It is not all tragedy. It is also beauty and recovery.
Such color on the foothills. Such Italian expressions for ground—
verdaccio, imprimatura.

Rain is the preferred condition, life in the rushes.
Which we cannot penetrate without consent of its invisible rulers.
The blackbird song pink, often heard in metaphor.

To be transparent is to be seen, to have blackbirds pass through.
Not a glass that stoppers, not glassine,
which resists, but as the eyes can make their way through light.

Here is a score for brief soloists. Matches lit and blown out.
Of a piece that snags and tears and gets rewoven.
One cannot speak of blackbird and not mean thirteen—the male

colony piping, the females quieter, among leaves, brown cattail
casings overwintered.
Thunder this morning. Geese raise their necks from the blue

bunch wheat grass they sleep in. Sky world. Our beloved terrestrial.
In between, a middle realm.
Where the blackbirds will lay their eggs in an outstretched hand.

THE GOLDFINCH PEOPLE

After four days of storm, the lane is strewn with rags.
Sodden leaves and broken trim.

You could have stayed hidden, protected at the roots.
Instead, laughter. Yellow confetti.

You thrill. You thin that verb, trilling it.
Half an ounce, two. You throw yourselves into weather

as I tried to do, head-down, the gusts unbalancing
my gait, worried about the straining sounds above me.

Saffron stripe in greenery. You wear.
You are worn. Gladly, you present yourselves to others.

Is it possible to abandon my own syntax? Has the writing
of prose been overlong?

You flock to the little aspen outside the window
of the philistine. What invitation means: a smile for one.

A woman's body suffers from drink, from age.
I often tumble from the visual landscape because of it.

You make something happen by lifting it.
There is in you a showy joy. And so what if you show off,

flushed from the field by the powers that be—*alla prima!*
You exploit all your brightness at once.

You are direct, you are direction. Unpeeled from the wing.
You might get too close to people and things.

It will be all right when you return to your separate selves.
Once you're adored, once you've let yourselves be loved.

THE WIND PEOPLE AGAIN

I thought prevailing meant most likely, even predictably so,
    yet italicized, in ongoing arrival.
Not this wurthering, northwest overruling east.
    No intervals, and if there were, too thin for shelter.

She who loves the wind opens all her windows to it.
    Her house is cleared of furniture.
The carpeting is new. There is the scour and spotless emptiness
    of running water.

But sometimes there is the need to place what one has gathered,
    to close the doors, as well as to open them.
To sit down among one's finds. Perhaps what memory is,
    its clearest function.

In the swept space between outcrops, in this circle I found
    of stones, which seemed a weight to keep the earth from flying
—it is soul I am talking about. That story again.
    Animated, by which I mean self-steering.

Pink stone, yellow stone. Chunks of milky quartz.
    They are beautiful because someone has chosen them.
If deer were my soul, they would gaze down
    on me sitting here. If wind, it would form a cape behind me.

IV.

ANOTHER LETTER TO THE SOUL

1.

Texture of the soul: soft as smoked buckskin. A hand of fresh tobacco, almost three feet long, its leaves moist and pressed together, a darkened gold. The bundles at the winter ceremonies are never quite unfurled: clothing of the dead, soiled from oil on skin and within them the sacred charms and herbs. Perhaps the soul, as opposed to spirit, really is of the earth. Soul as something that surrounds us, which we grow into. My friend Lois says each person is divided into four parts, according to her Dakota tradition. Diaspora of the interior—spirit, shadow, soul, and mind—and our bodies, the hibernacula where they all rest. Perhaps the soul *is* the body, which ages, which causes pain, which exhausts itself with its own caretaking. Mother bent over the heart stove, washing her husband's underarms and balls. The mornings backing up. Evenings spreading.

2.

A lowing, a rumble, something we might reach into, or catch under the black waves, or stumble over. Soul calls a halt to things, makes us stay where we are. I stay here amidst my lost opportunities. Lost opportunity to be with my mother in her decline. Why is she declining? Why can't she come to me? I read that rats will forego food to help another escape, scientific proof that mammals exhibit compassion. Females will do this almost one hundred percent, and males will do so, too, but much less often. When the rebels found their dictator hiding in a water pipe, someone rammed a steel pole up his rectum. What happens to the soul when someone does this? The soul, veined and folded, read in harsh light. Like a church full of votives burning through the night, almost imperceptibly going out one by one.

3.

In the garden, slivers and coins of stone surface. I pick them from the thinnest stem of chard. Clouds a luxury in dry lands drifting over us. Clouds that shadow other clouds. To be master of the invisible and yet be everywhere in plain sight. To *be* memory. To express the length of it. Violent rains, and yet this morning, the tiny siskin are in the lawn, feeding atop the seed heads of the dandelions. Dear soul that seems so root in us, everything has seeped out. You are a heavy silence, although you are a permeable one. Does soul equal soil? You must be a tensile skin we use to see within, but who sees out? If one is to be medium, one must be between two things, the dead and their audience, light and growth of leaf. One establishes one's privacies, and there you are. Empty boat bobbing through summer drift. Empty boat banging against the dock.

4.

Between each note, the composer tells me, are ten tones distinguishable by the human ear. The word Lake. Even better, the words Rose Lake. Carpets of *spring beauty*, what the Persians wove into their rugs. White star-clusters along the path we have come to climb. Do we grow into the soul as a plant does into air? The composer is talking now about the physiology of the inner ear, the drum, its thin membrane stretched as if to collect dust, the three bones behind it that, in turn, are struck: hammer, anvil, and stirrup. Imagine two streams, he says, running parallel, which is easy to do, since the snowmelt is next to us, rumbling over stones, creating a transparence that seems glassy and new. Imagine the ear as a wetted cloth the stream streams through. And soul, does it shine, or is it register of shine, of velocity, distance, algae, silt, and time? Wind, here in the mountains, slopes in silk miles. A sound we empty and a sound we fill.

V.

THE HAWK PEOPLE

THE HAWK PEOPLE

It screamed in the wilderness way we do,
chilling the first time you hear it, then addicting,
something you seek.

To perch above old age, the withering loss
of disease, or whatever might
come into the field, though not yet visible.

Until you are struck by an emptiness
that is full of the past—all those who have left,
whom your friend calls *the majority*.

The hawk screamed until you didn't go away.
Though it is always more dangerous when silent.
Restive cipher, conveyor of the dead.

When it lunged at the glass, stopping just short
of crashing into it,
glass was metaphor for not feeling, for distance.

Though fear flew through you, its chemical flash.
Sharp stars
in the inexorably dark tunnel of the body.

The hawk appears above the meadow, the forest,
along the industrial shore, scouting
the opening pockets of the psychic continuum.

To take the hawk and see your whole life through it
would be means to accept its power.
As vision, as the transparence between animals.

MANITOU

Out there, burrowed in the straw and snow of streambed, nosing itself up at first light. Its fur, fish-scaled with hoarfrost. The clicks and jingle of its rise. Not like a monster but rather the weak blue above the ridge, calling forth nothing but the wood getters, the rumble of their old trucks, overfilled, ready to spill in the ruts, a hard way to make a poor living. A quarter of calf-kills are by mountain lions, not the gray wolf though wolf is the one most hated. It has legs and is tiger-striped with low beams. It wears the shattered skin of ancient moons. The Manitou must be appealed to, must be placed inside the web of our growing feather debts and obligations. Soon, the mammoth, the short-faced bear. In that cold expensive city of our birth. So cold the smoke hangs straight down from its hooks. Chickadees pile together in the woodpecker's hole, an anxiety inside the heart of every tree. Though it was once colder. Our voices would ring out against the glass of air, the water sound come slow like ghosts walking across the fields, and *seem* was a seam between us.

THE LAKE PEOPLE

The silver electricity of the current
that joins one lake to another
below the surface
in which we can see at noon
the mountains on three sides,
their true, their upside down nature.

You move far from me, I watch you
enter, traverse the ridge.
The winds pick up,
clouds sink under the busy water.

Between first sleep and second sleep,
a few hours of drift,
when we can resist the push to live
the life we dictate.

Waves flatten and loom, and it begins
to rain, each drop large
as a quarter, a foot apart, each splash
the material equivalent of reflection.
A magic shining church of visible bells.

Under the primary sunlight, moonlight,
the hierarchs of division:
the various months and stars, countries
with their changing names and borders.

There are bonds between people
that can be loosened. When I was young,
the psychics called them cords.
Dangerous, how easily
we can return to who we were before,
fade back to our original sequences.

THE MEADOWLARK PEOPLE

and you begin to sing—and I am disappearing
—GENNADY AYGI

I achieve it simply, writing 'you' and 'I,'
inaugurating appearance with disappearance. I went
to bed. The young people had a fire.
You begin to sing and I become irrelevant.

Sheep shine in the distance. Up close, a dirty gray.
Who else but lambs could be described as frolicking?
Whitetail does are dancers, pointing
toes as they leap. They are not herds but families.

The composer is explaining that Arco means to bow.
All musical direction takes flight from the Italian.
Blue heron from water, horned lark from the green,
the sparrows measuring the level of the furrows.

H.D. stumbled at the podium, someone caught her,
and eros flared. Of course, she was humiliated by it.
Wind between her fingers, like the slipping off
of wedding rings, bitter tea of old age in her stomach.

We are lucky to have had lovers, how they decorate
our rooms. Light returns, longing for intensity—
the so-what of true feeling, to be responsive as the deer,
running because the meadow is wide enough.

THE SWALLOWTAIL PEOPLE

A cloud passes over you and I forget the sun; it comes back and you revive, a state of wonder. Luminosity and complete collapse, tumbling down onto the path but usually able to get up again. You are like watching a glittered creature, one from the myth, which has slipped with the moths into their cocoons, sleep spun around you in gossamer but sturdy threads, and yet here you are gesturing of flight again. Behaviorism, they say, posits that if we want to believe, we act like we believe and eventually we will. If we act ritualistic, we become ritual. If we act like we have all the time in the world. The creek in spring is gathering its chorus, a lot of by-hand shorthand and hourly touch. You say: we remember people by the feeling we once felt for them. Intermediate creatures, remnants left of wind, much is lost off the edge of your dreams. Like the swallowtail in February you pulled from the snow, still soaked in its supernatural beams. Animal tales: we make them up as we enter them, blue eye-spots on the wings, blue continuous all around the outer margins. Lemon-yellow and horizontal, and much like birds.

AUGUST DEER

Skill at sighting animals develops in the mountains—
a shift in magnetism, a displacement of air,

melon texture turned temperature, an under-brightness.
As all creatures can sense the gaze of another.

If you want to see ghosts, look down the long valley
at dusk. This is also when the waters begin to talk.

Shimmer: the rhyme between *given* and *again*.
What can I find in the shadows there?

To work as a direct expression of inner calling—
not the material, but *material,* the inherited talents,

pacing of the deer, excluding panic.
Mastery of transition, pause. When we go no further.

Quieted. Enigmatic, as in not having
to explain. Like a breeze, not wishing harm to anyone.

Their gentleness, their watery light, their sleep that is
itself relief from sleeplessness: the deer

stand at the field edge, in the shallow colors of dawn,
having browsed there, having clearly intervened.

VI.

ANOTHER LETTER TO THE SOUL

*After a series of photographs of Kazuo Ohno
taken by Eikoh Hosoe, Hokkaido, Japan, 1994*

1.

I watch the Butoh dancer fall layer by layer through the worlds until the floor becomes a barrier to the last one. He wears a dilapidated hat, made of twig and straw, as if a magpie nest were constructed atop his head. *A great many people are coming to life in me,* he says. Like the minerals of earth inside my blood. Who lives in our bodies? Who passes through? What ghost dances *ghost-dances* in our thoughts? In the series of transformations—the operation, the fire, the night I poisoned myself eating wild mushrooms from the field—there was danger, but something always woke me up. The soul must be transparent, a teardrop made of glass, like the crystal I found detached from its chandelier. Hung in my window here, it releases rainbow flock after flock, which land momentarily on my blankets or my hands. *What about your hands,* the dancer says, *use them more freely.* As if they grew those selves inside them and sent them out.

2.

The human soul: waist deep in ferns, in fiddlehead. In frond. About face. In agony. The wounded figure is sinking beautifully, like a girl into sleep—mouth open, eyes half closed, hand larger than his face, raised above it as if resting on a pillow. Hair, as if staggered with straw. And look, earth is eating him. The body succumbs, falling to its knees, but no longer screaming. The sound is of birds leaving, a wind farther back, behind the trees, the temperature just tipping toward discomfort. Body melting like a candle in heat. A suicide is always chosen, perhaps even a graceful way to die, but are we not meant to go through this, the diminishment and pain? As of a blanket slipping off a shoulder. As of days clear as water of event. I can feel it in the landscape: this is where one of us went down. The spot wherein one of us has given up.

3.

How strange, how strangely furtive the species looks without clothes, holding in front of it, as if something breakable, its precious hands. Look, it is in the water now, has taken shape as a twisted tree. Suddenly upright, its pitiful organs exposed. To see ourselves as prey in landscape, watched by something larger, with larger jaws, caught eating, caught stealing, caught *unbeautiful*. What we might look like when death is taking over: half-bird, half-animal, featherless, without wings, the hides of what we have killed draped over us. Perhaps the dark horizon is not really storm-filled but rather the dawn overcoming night, when the figure must find the opening out of which it crawled. Perhaps the light hurts its eyes, and it is blinded.

4.

In this photograph, the view is from a distance, and it is not clear whether the figure is there or not, as is often true with the non-figurative. Not in the uncut grass, grown so tall it has folded over. Not in the bow or bend of the river, smooth as a road of snow, not snow because the bank reeds are reflected in it. Storm, where we are, ready to take over there. He could be anywhere, under any tree, already buried by the hay. He could be landscape with suffering hiding in it. Because when we try hard and each time we are thwarted, we think we might wait a while, here off the path, with everyone else oblivious, speeding up. Looking forward, is that what is finally taken away from us? The figure prowls like the heron along a weeded shore. Strange as the mind that distinguishes us.

VII.

THE CREEK PEOPLE

THE CREEK PEOPLE

Rain, one syllable. Multiplied, like a mood.
Creek predominate, the cool bottom of the rain.

My calling seems close, perhaps because of leisure,
as if I were here only to witness it.

As if—between a question and its answers,
none of them wrong. Rain, as if it will save us.

An edge people, a transition species.

I cannot halt this acceleration toward death—
mother, father, sisters sucked up into it.

All change is toward healing. Though it may look
misguided, even pathological.

To see is to go out to see. The creek sobs the winter.
I should, too, with my sugar-coated eyes.

Consciousness and its opposite, forgetfulness.

I sleep with my mind closed to it, though ears
never close. When I wake, birthday of the vase flower.

The creek shrinks under ice and emerges in the spring
enlarged. *The flesh*, as Merleau-Ponty calls it.

A lock of sheep's wool stretched into
diaphanous fibers, fine, almost breakable clouds.

Accidents, the unfortunate already gone.

THE BACKYARD NEST

Commonplace, featherless, pink, all beak, without any muscle tone to speak of. Their nest, in the lilac bush, next to the kale and dill, so public and central I kept brushing against it. Worm-eaters. It seems incongruous, the privilege of their turquoise eggs or their dulcet voices, earliest and last on summer lawns. I am sure that no one pointed out robin song when I was young. I had to learn to match my happiness to it. The hatching, the helplessness, the flat downy pile, the long weeks of deliquescence, the appearance of eyes. And then vanished into elsewhere, while I stay here. Look, we have found each other late. We might be running out of time. I say yes to whatever you want to do. Peering through the leafage, perhaps getting too close, I am alert for the least sign of weakness. A friend tells me she has decided to interpret every sign as good, a hermeneutic that might take years to practice. The robins, for instance. The shock they won't return. How often I find myself still peering in after them.

THE PATH THROUGH THE FOREST

Age-old genesis of light and shadow,
the various greens hidden or revealed between them,
lace of grouse whortleberry,
the berries now gone. Or say *hiding*, which gives green volition.
The most silent of men pass us
on horseback, down from their dawn hunt,
an elk's head strapped between their saddlebags on top.
Meat bleeding quietly through the linen.
It's beautiful in my direction; is it in yours?
Lake water flashing its dark eyes at us.
It goes to sleep, as we do, reciting the countless names of blue.
It dreams in vestibules cool and fragrant.
New snow on the near slopes, wool darkening in pouring rain.
We are nearing the end of the flower corridor.
The world becomes smaller, more northern, with age.
The new skills less important for us to learn.
Deer emerge from the wrinkles in thickets with still tiny fawns.
Bless them. That they will harden before the deep cold.
That the fall will be soft, as if into oregano.
In the pockets of early winter, the carpenters sent home,
the false mornings dark with the lamps on,
we will remember how it felt to break through
what we knew, the body left behind to its delirium.

BONE YARD

There is an earth below the body, white gleam in what is other-
wise sage. You are unafraid, even curious at death now. Ravens pick
through the catalogs. In their beaks, the redbrown stain. They hang,
a glossy black in the greening house. Today, you walk right into the
bone yard, recognizing first a shod hoof. The ribcage further on, the
long neck spreading. What is strewn like feathers is hair caught in
last year's grass. We can almost make out an ear. A stillborn calf?
A deer? But you, you say, have had enough now. We return to the
farmer's field of right and wrong. Widow's weeds, or the heavy cur-
tains that signal to the neighbors the house is closed: these are grief
rules few of us know any longer. Shall we say he was released? Did
he step out of his mind or was he flung? We have followed the path
back to the river, where you cast river pebbles from shore, as if it
were up to you to send him on. We watch them sink, the force of
gravity much too strong.

A SCHOOL FOR GIRLS

Willow, with its bright yellow belly and gray green wings,
and its sister warbler, offered something she shines in.

To be a friend is to be alive together. *Not relationship but bond,*
to step out from one's valence with outstretched hand.

A screen door unlatched, balancing half-open in the breeze—
we don't know what death is, what's inside it.

But let us keep the conversation going. I called this listening
in the past. Now I open gifts only when others are around me.

The book of feathers includes clouds
in their hanging world, the distinct features of a wisdom society.

Written by leaves in summer is the book of silk,
raven wings scripted on air. A sound as of making an impression.

Narrow and shaded backyard of the *anthropocene* home,
"back" as in out the back door. Where, at night, we light sparklers.

Today, the hunters say the elk are all hiding under rocks.
Hunting season, like football season, when men are at their worst,

says the Great Mother of the Animals.
The two black moose that stand in front of us as if outside time.

Intimidated easily, longing for delight, a quick temper
when others are wronged—so few clothes to be worn through

a life, to be passed on. *Take her hands,* the women say when
I am overwhelmed with grief, aphorism in the list we divvy up.

THE FROZEN CREEK PEOPLE

Near the house, the horse-clop of tire chains. The mountain, like my childhood, a figure shadowed behind a curtain of snow. *Life is everything,* Sontag protested, before leaving it. To see through an absence as one sees the water through the holes in ice. I miss the dead as far as I can remember them, far as generations have remembered for me. Atop the ice, hundreds of frost flowers cut out from cold air. Like talking to my mother the afternoon of her recent illness. A weightlessness on the surface, small and clawed. Certain places in the driveway, the silence of the creek exerts itself. Like a god suddenly rumbling at high speed around the bend. And the heart pounds as it does, its solitude devastated. *To record the unknown surfacing in our time.* The creek comes down from the mountain to stand in front of itself. Will I disappear when my mother no longer sees me? Ghost problem. Death as variant. Three chickadees like fingertips in my hair.

VIII.

ANOTHER LETTER TO THE SOUL

1.

The mule deer, when they spot me on the still-bare ridge, line up in single file at the fence, disappearing into earth-tone with snow-patch on their rumps, invisible until the first one leaps. Thought: a small moment. We are made and unmade. The bone smuggler knows fossils are just rocks. Why should we claim paleontology as so important? Wind crosses in front of me, jangling the gate, making the tree caught in another's limbs moan and shift, igniting a flare down the road. I love winter, have loved so many winters. At this point, my life seems overlong. The ruffed grouse that star-tles into its loud twig-snap flight leaves me with its heart-thunder below. What is left when spirit flees us and the soul is decomposed? Forked feet and belly-drag of her curious chain-link track. *Suicide bomber* and *drone* added to the Webster's.

2.

Soul stress: the clanging of a bell in the strong winds of the eastern front or an avalanche in the snowmobile exhaust's wake. The weather unchaining, a slow coming apart. Hairline cracks widening in the vase. Over the phone, my friend's breathing sounds ragged, evaporative. As if it he were thinning to air. My soul is dizzy, he says. What to call this? Precarious structure, like the soil, disintegrating in the rain? Weakness? Pathopsychology? There is horror in what humans do, and the sensitives, those like you, whose hands sometimes tremble, who have no spleens, having lost them in the accidents of childhood, suddenly see auras and must sit down. Just beyond the normalcy of everyday life: *the flammable face of the world.* The mind, at the edge, just an organ. Its bluster and dying down. Its retina, a shattered piece of glass.

3.

Where in the body is the soul today? "Anatomy," not "astronomy."
Look this morning at the deer, sleeping on its side in a pile of leaves.
Put yourself there, under the stars. Protected, really, from nothing.
Having to trust the air. Or gray solitaire on the bare branch of the
extreme cold. Where outside the body is the soul today? It will seem
as if it is happening all around you. As if the sun had moved into a
new phase. Pale, breathless, a bottomless blue, a sentimental cro-
chet of clouds at the edgework. The woman who made her friends
promise not to parade her in public after she lost her mind found
such joy in the choir that they were torn. Which is a feeling you
have forgotten. Hope, one might say. The tilting that is change on
the axis. If there is someone in the wind, there is someone in the
mountain. If the soul is back there, in the child that was harmed, it
is also in the older girl who takes her hand. Leading her through the
burning trees, which breathe out emeralds.

4.

Asked to describe the soul, some will say a flame, some an orb. No one mentions the basement apartment. No one says the sick-room, its artificial light. Soul, being a journey, which sometimes gets stuck in place. Barreling or feeding like a silkworm through space, outgrowing itself again in its fifth instar. How to facilitate this, so death comes not as tragedy but as if ministered by girls, whose hands move over the belly, the thighs, adjusting the night-clothes. Their hearts, which might be most alive when broken. Poor, agitated pupa. Crawling out of its skin. Spared: only those who dwell most inland. There is a film flickering from a crack in the earth that those, who are caretaking, witness. Splashed with it, irradiated, their focus shifts. Bring back the dying to ice water in tin cups, butter their dry faces. And if this discomforts—the soul bulky, even obscene, as if it were wearing something intimate too large—sit like a god would and watch them go through it.

5.

Hung on a frame under the tent of healing, we walk and the vials tinkle like a hundred jostled bells: ginger for the tender stomach, Oxycontin for the tender soul, and buckets of Ambien for the sleepless. It is safer, it seems, wiser, to encounter one's friends above the earth. To remember also the restorative power of silence. A river that has frozen over can still carve a narrow stream where a colloquy of polytheism is spoken. A literature can permeate, like water does, the hidden regions where human influence does not extend, past the ancestral suburbs, under and through touch. Something we might call a change of mind. So many days of caretaking—building fires, making ice, slipping the brandy stoppers under the tongue—even the most hardened criminals are softened by proof of good within them. A feeling which might begin in the form of rain.

6.

Welcome, first snow, I speak into the dark. There is the early morning shuffle of its apparel. The slide of buttons, as of a coat slipped off. A friend tells me, if we could see spirit, it would be this flame-blue. I used to think so, too, but then I dreamt it. If spirit rises long-tailed, a magpie with iridescent wings, does soul sink back to be melted and molded and made new again? The soul, then, as under construction? We are in a bed in the upstairs of a house in the making. It is the reading season. No one on the road. The towns seeming further away. And the young? Are we less interested in what they're doing? *Tell me which infinity attracts you,* Bachelard writes, *and I will know the meaning of your world.* I am afraid of the ocean, and now fire, and, though I would like to know the sky, I am drawn to the infinity that is earth. Rock, its own shape, own meaning, not ours. The weight-bearing, sun burnt character of its slopes.

NOTES & ACKNOWLEDGMENTS

Grateful acknowledgment to the editors of the journals who published the following poems, sometimes with different titles and in different form:

Basalt: "The Meadowlark People," "The Deer People," "The Frozen Creek," "The Creek People"

Concis Magazine: "Swallowtail," "Bone Yard"

Copper Nickel: "The Red-Winged Blackbird People," "The Wind People"

Dark Matter: Women Witnessing: "Another Letter to the Soul": [You picked me from the litter], [The watercolorists], [Water. Mint.]

Field: "Another Letter to the Soul": [Soul stress], [The mule deer, when they spot me], [Where in the body is the soul today], [Asked to describe the soul]

Gulf Coast: "Another Letter to the Soul": [You are the story of my love in ruins], [You are the sound of rain], [I am working out the days of the week]

High Desert Journal: "The Cottonwood People"

Kenyon Review: "Another Letter to the Soul": [I watch the Butoh dancer], [The human soul: waist deep], [How strange, how strangely furtive], [In this photograph]

Knockout: "The Path Through the Forest," "The Lake People"

Pleiades: "The Pronghorn Antelope People"

Stringtown: "August Deer," "Goldfinch People," "The Hawk People," "Another Letter to the Soul": [Asked to describe the soul], "The Backyard Nest"

Talking River: "A School for Girls," "The Deer People Again," "The Hide and Skin Handbook"

The Journal: "Manitou"

Willow Springs: "Another Letter to the Soul": ([Texture of the soul], [A lowing, a rumble], [In the garden, slivers], [Between each note], [Hung on a frame]

"The Pronghorn Antelope People" and "The Cottonwood People" also appear in *Poems Across the Big Sky II: An Anthology of Montana Poets*, edited by Lowell Jaeger and Hannah Bissell (Kalispell, MT: Many Voices Press, 2016).

A suite of poems from "Another Letter to the Soul" was performed in collaboration with jazz musician M. J. Williams, February 2016, at 1+1 Gallery in Helena, Montana.

◊   ◊   ◊

I am grateful to the Ucross Foundation for a residency at which drafts of many of these poems were written.

In "A School for Girls," I am indebted to Lois Red Elk for the words *Take her hands* and the story behind them, which appear in her book *Dragonfly Weather*. Thank you, Lois.

Many thanks to Christopher Howell, whose marvelous poem "Another Letter to the Soul" was the first inspiration for this book.

ABOUT THE AUTHOR

Melissa Kwasny is the author of six collections of poems, including *Pictograph, Reading Novalis in Montana*, and *The Nine Senses*, which contains a set of poems that won the Poetry Society of America's 2009 Cecil Hemley Memorial Award. A portion of *Pictograph* received the society's 2009 Alice Fay Di Castagnola Award, judged by Ed Roberson. Kwasny's nonfiction book, *Putting on the Dog: Animals and Our Clothing*, is forthcoming from Trinity University Press, and she is author of the essay collection *Earth Recitals: Essays on Image and Vision*. She has edited multiple anthologies, including *Toward the Open Field: Poets on the Art of Poetry, 1800–1950* and, with M. L. Smoker, *I Go to the Ruined Place: Contemporary Poems in Defense of Global Human Rights*. Widely published in journals and anthologies, Kwasny's work has appeared in *Ploughshares, Boston Review*, and *The Arcadia Project: North American Postmodern Pastoral*. She lives outside of Jefferson City, Montana, in the Elkhorn Mountains.